THE GROSS OUT CONTINUES

Why is pregnancy in Hollywood so magical?

The minute a starlet knows she's pregnant, the father disappears!

_____

What happened to the leper who walked into a screen door?

He strained himself!

_____

Where do masochists meet?

At a smack bar!

_____

A new collection of the most outrageous, hysterical, and far-out humor from America's best-selling funny man

JULIUS ALVIN

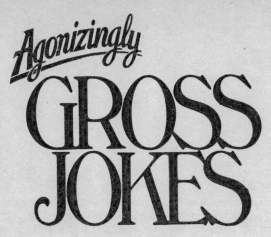

Agonizingly GROSS JOKES

Volume IX

By Julius Alvin

ZEBRA BOOKS
KENSINGTON PUBLISHING CORP.

ZEBRA BOOKS

are published by

Kensington Publishing Corp.
475 Park Avenue South
New York, NY 10016

First printing: July, 1990

Printed in the United States of America

TABLE OF CONTENTS

Chapter One

Gross Racial and Ethnic Jokes

What happens when twelve black jurors are assigned to a Ku Klux Klan trial?

You get a hung jury.

How can you tell a Sicilian town is small?

It has a grandmother instead of a godfather.

Why did the Polack throw six puppies in the garbage can?

The sign said, "Place litter here."

———————————

How did the hard-of-hearing Polack ruin the furniture?

Someone told him "Sit in the chair."

———————————

Why are so many black kids illegitimate?

Black men don't breed well in captivity.

———————————

Two Polacks from Chicago decided to try the sport of hunting. They drove a few hours to northern Wisconsin and found a hunting lodge. The lodge owner rented them guns, ammunition, clothing, boots, then said, "You'll also need some dogs. I'll let you have three of my best."

The Polacks thanked him, then headed into the woods. The lodge owner was surprised to see them at the door less than an hour later. "Sorry," the Polacks said. "But we need some more dogs."

"Why? Those were my best dogs."

"They were good," the Polacks said. "But we've already shot them."

———————————

What do you get when you cross a black and a Jew?

A kid who feels guilty about being on welfare.

———————————

Did you hear about the Olympic weightlifter who took steroids?

He had so much in him that he had to be classified as an East German woman.

———————————

A Polack was sitting in a bar when the bartender said, "Hey, want to hear a joke?"

The Polack grimaced. "No way. I'm sick of Polish jokes. I'll only listen to a joke that doesn't involve me in any way."

"You want to hear something that has nothing to do with you?"

"Yeah," the Polack replied.

"Your wife is pregnant," the bartender said.

Did you hear about the enterprising rabbi who opened a storefront circumcision business?

He calls it The Clip Joint.

Why is it such a good business?

Every customer leaves a tip.

What's a Swedish call girl?

A smorgasbroad.

Why don't Polish girls ever drown?

Even the tide won't take them out.

Did you hear that the Solidarity Union finally persuaded the Polish government to give in to their demands?

They got longer hours and shorter pay.

———————

What did the Warsaw city government do when a bridge needed repair?

Called in a team of dentists.

———————

What is automation?

It's a process of making work so easy even Mexicans can do it.

———————

What do you get when you cross a Chinaman with a Jewish mother?

Someone who bakes misfortune cookies.

How can you tell a woman has a serious weight problem?

She shaves her armpits before she steps on the scale.

How can you tell if the woman is Italian?

After she shaves, she's five pounds lighter.

Did you hear about the Puerto Rican kid who was too young to drive?

He stole taxis.

What do you give a Polish girl that goes along with her looks?

Horse shoes.

How can you tell if an Irishman found a $10 bill?

Smell his breath.

How much do Irishmen spend on liquor?

A staggering amount.

———————————

What's Irish arthritis?

You get stiff in a new joint every night.

———————————

What's an Irishman's idea of a balanced diet?

A drink in each hand.

———————————

What did the Polack do when his car needed a new muffler?

Went home and started knitting one.

What's a Polish M.D.?

"Mentally Deficient."

———————

Why did the Polack take a ruler to bed?

He wanted to see how long he slept.

———————

Why was the Italian guy exhausted every morning?

He spent all night running around his bed trying to catch some sleep.

———————

What's the difference between an Italian and a Polack?

A Polack eats with his hands and talks with his fork.

What's a Scottish wedding bouquet?

A packet of seeds.

———————————

Did you hear about the lonely Puerto Rican?

He robbed a bank so he could feel wanted.

———————————

What are pipe dreams to a kid in Harlem?

Growing up to be a crack dealer.

———————————

Did you hear about the new Polish wonder product?

Artificial dandruff for people who wear wigs.

Did you hear about the other Polish wonder product?

Waterproof tea bags.

What's the only way to get a JAP hot?

Cremation.

––––––––––––––––

What's the best way to keep a JAP happy?

Give her a lot of credit.

––––––––––––––––

What's the one advantage of marrying a Polish girl?

In twenty years, she'll be just as pretty as she is on her wedding day.

––––––––––––––––

What's a formal hillbilly wedding?

The shotgun's painted white.

What do you know if a guy walks into your store with a stocking over his head?

He's either a robber or he's Polish.

_____

What four things are preprinted on a Polack's checks?

Name, address, phone number, and "Insufficient Funds."

_____

What's birth control to an Italian wife?

Making it all the way to the delivery room.

_____

Why do so many black girls miss the first day of junior high school?

Morning sickness.

How can you tell you're leafing through a Polish first reader?

Jane's a dog, too.

What's the difference between a white parent and a black parent?

When a white parent wants to check his kid's marks, he looks at his report card; when a black parent wants to check his kid's marks, he rolls up his sleeve.

A Polish guy was sitting at the bar when he noticed a good-looking woman staring at him. Finally, she came over and said, "Hey, handsome, how about giving me your telephone number?"

"You don't need to write it down. It's in the telephone book," the Polack replied.

"Well, what's your name?" she asked.

"That's in the phone book, too," the Polack said.

Two Irishmen had finished all the booze in the house and were rumbling through the closet looking for something more to drink. One held up a bottle and slurred, "Hey, Pat, how about this stuff?"

"Can't you read?" the second Irishman replied. "On the side in big letters it says, 'Poison.'"

"That's just to throw us off," the first Irishman said as he hoisted it to his lips. "On this side, it says 'Lye.'"

———————

Why does it take two stewardesses to serve every meal on El Al Airlines?

One passes out the food, the other goes around going, "Eat, eat!"

———————

Why was the black guy so interested in his family tree?

His family was still living in it.

Why do Italian soldiers always drop their rifles and run away?

Because they can't fly.

———————

What's the most popular black antiperspirant?

Unemployment.

———————

How do we know that all black kids are spoiled?

One whiff and you can tell.

———————

A Polack walked into the bar one night wearing a suit and tie instead of his usual overalls. One of his astounded buddies said, "Hey, Stash. What's with the new clothes?"

The Polack beamed. "My wife got them for me."

What was the occasion?"

"I don't know," he replied. "I came home from work early yesterday, and there they were, hanging over the chair in our bedroom."

How can you tell a Polish housewife in the supermarket?

She's squeezing the canned pears to see if they're fresh.

Did you hear about the Polish woman who gave birth on the bus?

The cops arrested her for littering.

Why did the Polack name his son Effigy?

He knew he'd be a dummy when he grew up.

What's a Polish permanent?

Wet your finger, then stick it in a light socket.

A Polack walked into the bar and ordered up a round of drinks for his friends. "What's the occasion?" they asked.

"I'm a lucky man," the Polack replied. "I never realized how much my wife loved me until I had to stay home from work sick the other day."

"So what did she do?"

"She was so happy to have me home," he said, "that every time someone came to the door, like the mailman and the milkman, she'd shout 'My husband's home! My husband's home!'"

What's the toughest thing about being a Polish parent?

Going down every week to buy your kid back from the dogcatcher.

How did the WASP kid know his parents hated him?

They hired an actor to play him in home movies.

A Polack went to see the doctor and said, "I need some help losing weight. Nothing I try seems to work."

"I should be able to help you," the doctor replied. "But before I give you a weight-loss plan, I have to know what your diet is like now. I want you to keep a record of everything you eat for a week."

The Polack agreed. One week later, he walked back into the doctor's office and showed him his tie.

———————

What's the benefits of marrying a Mexican?

An unlimited supply of natural gas.

———————

A black guy was walking along the road in rural Mississippi when a police car stopped. Two hulking white policemen grabbed the guy, handcuffed him, rapped him a few times with their nightsticks, and tossed him in the back of the patrol car.

A couple of hours later, the black dude was sitting in a cell in the county jail when the sheriff walked in. "What am I here for?" the black guy asked. "I didn't do nothing."

"Boy," the sheriff said, "Bubba told me you were resisting arrest. You go to trial, Judge Carter'll send you up for ten years hard time."

"But I didn't do anything," the black guy said.

"Don't back talk to me, boy," the sheriff said. "You be a good nigger, and I'll tell you what. You plead guilty, and I'll see you get a suspended sentence."

The black guy agreed. So they took him out and hanged him.

———————

Why aren't disposable diapers a problem in Harlem?

In Harlem, the mothers dispose of their babies.

———————

What's the best way to find out if there's life after death?

Go for a walk in Harlem.

Did you hear about the Polish stripper?

The crowd kept shouting, "Up in front!"

Did you hear about the Polish go-go girl?

Every time a man saw her, he'd shout, "Go! Go!"

_____

Did you hear about the Polish scientist who thought he'd invented a cure for impotency?

It backfired, and gave him piles.

_____

What happened when a guy gave an Irishman a hotfoot?

It took three days to put the flames out.

_____

Did you hear about the Polack who hijacked a submarine?

He asked for ten million dollars and a parachute.

How do Polacks cure brain tumors?

Preparation H.

———————

What's an ambitious Polack?

A man who knows what he wants, but can't spell it.

———————

What ethnic group has the lowest longevity?

JAPs—you'll never find one over 40.

———————

How do we know that JAPs are kind to animals?

They'll do anything for a mink.

Why did the Italian kid wear a coffin for a hat?

His teacher told him he was dead from the neck up.

———————

What's worse than trying to sell ice to Eskimos?

Selling Father's Day cards in Harlem.

What's worse than trying to sell ice to Eskimos?

Being a mind reader in Poland.

———————

What's the only way to keep an Italian from smelling?

Cut off his nose.

———————

If Santa were Jewish, what would little girls get for Christmas?

A doll house with a mortgage on it.

How did the Scotsman save money on his honeymoon?

He went alone.

When will a Scotsman pick up a check?

When it's made out to him.

It was getting toward evening when an old black man shuffled into the small-town police station in Alabama and told the desk sergeant he wanted to report his friend missing.

"What happened?" the desk sergeant asked.

"Well, I was walking my friend Rufus down by the Decatur Highway. I be shuffling along when I heards a truck horn real loud. I gets off the side of the road to lets him go by. But then I can'ts see Rufus."

"Pop," the desk sergeant said, "maybe Rufus decided to take a nap."

"I don't know," the old black man said. "I keeps walking up the road. First I see old Rufus's arm in the ditch. Little ways up, there's his leg in a bush. After a while, I think maybe something's happened to him."

What's the advantage of firing a Polack?

You won't have a vacancy to fill.

———————

Why is it so bad when a JAP has PMS?

For a JAP, it stands for Permanent Mental State.

———————

What do you call an Italian with a war medal?

A thief.

———————

What do you call toxic waste dump?

A Polish health spa.

What's JAP aerobics?

You shop faster.

———————

Why did the Polack stand across the room from the telephone?

He was trying to make a long-distance call.

———————

How can you tell a Jewish tourist in Rome?

At the Fountain of Trevi, he tosses in a pledge.

———————

Who are the most ethical people in the world?

Puerto Ricans—every one is a man of conviction.

Did you hear about the Polish guy who got a job at a medical school?

He was a cadaver.

———————————

A woman was having lunch with a JAP friend when she said, "Bill is just impossible. Absolutely nothing pleases him. Tell me, is your Sydney hard to please?"

The JAP shrugged. "I wouldn't know. I've never tried."

———————————

The Jewish businessman hired a big handsome young black man as a chauffeur. The black dude was an excellent driver, but the businessman became a trifle worried about the way his wife looked at him. When it came time for the husband to go on a business trip, he told the chauffeur, "Jefferson, I don't want you anywhere near my wife while I'm away."

"Oh," Jefferson replied, "you don't have to worry about me, boss. A couple years ago, there were bullets flying on my block and one hit me right in my love machine."

The businessman extended his sympathy, but he was immensely relieved as he drove to the airport. Unfortunately, his flight was canceled, and he had to return home that night. To his shock, he walked into the bedroom to find Jefferson pumping away on his wife.

"Jefferson," he shouted. "I thought you told me that your thing had been shot off."

"It was," the black man said. "But it left a ten-inch stump."

A friend saw the Polack sitting dejectedly in the park. "Why are you so glum?" he asked.

"It's my dog," the Polack lamented.

"Did he die?"

"No. I took him to obedience school."

The friend was puzzled. "So what was the problem? Did he flunk out?"

"That's not it," said the Polack. "He learned to sit up and shake hands three days before I did."

Why did the Polack broil his shoe?

He wanted to serve filet of sole.

Why wouldn't the Polish lineman sign the million-dollar pro-football contract?

He wanted Sundays off.

How does a JAP get a mink?

The same way a mink gets a mink.

Who are the hardest-working municipal employees?

Italian garbagemen—every night they bring their work home with them.

When does an Irishman stagger home from the bar?

Whenever the spirits move him.

How can you tell when a WASP widow is in mourning?

She orders black olives with her martinis.

How come Polish girls are so quiet when they're screwing?

They don't believe in talking to strangers.

What's an old-fashioned Italian girl?

One with a handlebar mustache.

How do Italian girls shave their legs?

They lie down on the ground and have someone run over them with a lawn mower.

Question: "What's do-it-yourself acupuncture?"

Answer: "A Polack with a fork."

Why did the Polack have "$1.99" tatooed on his cheek?

He heard that all tough guys have a price on their heads.

What's the busiest time at a Harlem brothel?

Father and daughter night.

How can you tell if duck hunters are Polish?

The decoy gets away.

Did you hear about the Polish woman who wanted artificial insemination?

She went to bed with a robot.

———————

What do you call an Israeli sea captain?

Yom Skipper.

———————

What's an unmarked car?

One a JAP's never driven.

———————

How can you tell a junkie is Polish?

He's the one trying to put his pipe in his crack.

Did you hear about the JAP who forbade certain four-letter words to be used in her house?

They included, "cook," "wash," "dust . . ."

What's the rudest gift to send to a JAP?

A subscription to "Good Housekeeping."

What's the easiest way for an Italian to lose five pounds?

Clean his nails.

After years of working as a laborer, the Polack won the lottery. His first purchase was a big house with a heated swimming pool. He invited a few friends over on the day he moved in.

A butler met them at the door and escorted them to the pool. But they were astounded to see that the Polack was in his bathing suit but that the pool was dry. One guy turned to the Polack and said, "Haven't you filled the pool yet?"

"No," he said. "In fact, I told them to take the water out about an hour ago."

"Why would you do that?"

"Because," the Polack said as he walked out on the diving board, "I know how to dive, but I don't know how to swim."

––––––––––

Why is it so hard to convene a meeting of Polacks?

No matter where they meet, they're not all there.

––––––––––

Did you hear about the hillbilly who hated to see his wife scrubbing the wood floor of their cabin every day?

He took out the floor.

––––––––––

Did you hear that fourteen Mexicans were hurt in an accident?

Their bed collapsed.

What's a Harlem virgin?

A girl whose mother is too ugly to have a boyfriend.

Why is it easier to stock a fabric store for blacks?

If they have a choice, they'll always pick cotton.

What's the difference between a worm and an Irishman?

A worm doesn't fall down before he crawls home.

What's the most common type of public transportation in Harlem?

A hearse.

Paddy reeled out of bed in the morning and stumbled down to the kitchen. He had just poured a cup of coffee when he turned to see his wife glaring at him. The Irishman took a sip and snapped, "What's wrong with you? I was quiet when I came in last night."

His wife grimaced. "You didn't make any noise. But the four guys who carried you sure did."

———————————

What's different about an Italian hearse?

The coffin's empty and the body's in the trunk.

———————————

Did you hear about the Polish girl who didn't like the way she looked?

She walked into a tailor's shop and asked to have her birthday suit altered.

Two Jewish businessmen were talking after temple when one said, "Did you hear about our friend Sheldon?"

"What about him? How is business?"

"His business is no more. His warehouse burned to the ground last Thursday."

"Sheldon is such a great guy," the second Jew said. "Finally he got the good luck he deserves."

———————

Did you hear about the new Mexican-built sedan?

It comes in two models: ten passenger and twenty passenger.

———————

Exactly how distasteful did the JAP find sex?

She even had her guppies fixed.

Why did the Polack get kicked out of cooking school?

One morning his recipe began, "Get one frying pan. Then take a big leek . . ."

———————

What's the best way to get a black chick into the sack?

Slip her an Afro-disiac.

———————

Why did the Scotsman take up golf again after ten years?

He finally found his ball.

———————

Why aren't there many ethnic jokes about Englishmen?

It's dreary enough being English without making jokes about it.

What does a WASP wife say to her husband just before sex?

"Make sure you cover me after you're through."

_____

What did the Polish cop do when he heard about the bank robbery?

Called in for a description of the bank.

_____

Who are the most punctual women in the world?

JAPs—they buy everything on time.

_____

Why did the Polack put beer in his waterbed?

He wanted a foam mattress.

How do we know young black dudes are so religious?

They spend all their time preying.

Why was the Polish cop walking down the street wrapped in a blanket?

He was working undercover.

Chapter Two

Gross Celebrity Jokes

Why was Ronald Reagan the most efficient U.S. President?

Every day he got in eight hours work and eight hours sleep, and still had sixteen hours left over.

———————————

How can you tell if a person's a perfect candidate for Congress?

He's got the gift of grab.

What's the good news and the bad news about the eight years of the Reagan presidency?

The good news is that he led the nation to a position of world economic dominance; the bad news is, that nation was Japan.

How do we know Oedipus's mother was so open-minded?

She liked to do everything under the son.

Did you hear about the new Mike Tyson perfume for women?

You slap it on.

How dumb is Dan Quayle?

If you asked him what he thought, he'd be speechless.

Did you hear that Rosanne Barr diets religiously?

She never eats anything while she's in church.

———————

Why hasn't Warren Beatty ever married?

He's never found a woman who loves him as much as he does.

———————

What's Warren Beatty's idea of being unfaithful?

Turning away from the mirror.

———————

Did you hear that Dan Quayle finished his first book?

Reading it, not writing it.

Why is Dan Quayle like the Jolly Green Giant?

They're both prominent American vegetables.

Why are we lucky that there are evangelists on TV?

Before Jimmy Swaggart and Jim Bakker, a lot of people didn't really know what sin was.

Why is Dan Quayle so much in demand as a speaker?

Everyone loves to hear the inside dope.

How did Claus Von Bulow get rich?

It was just a lucky stroke.

What do you have when you have Don King and a pair of shoes?

Three heels.

_____

Why does George Bush have a clean conscience?

He's never used it.

_____

Why was Donald Trump so embarrassed?

He finally bounced a Czech.

_____

Why is Drexel Burnham Lambert like a football?

They both ended up in the hands of a receiver.

Did you hear about the new book about Drexel Burnham Lambert?

No matter where you open the book, you're in Chapter 11.

―――――――――

Did you hear that the Mets hired a naked call girl to parade around the bullpen?

They wanted their relief pitchers to warm up fast.

―――――――――

Why is Dan Quayle like a Jack-o'-lantern?

They're both heads with nothing inside.

―――――――――

Why did the United Nations send an Irish battalion to Beirut?

Irishmen are used to being bombed all day.

Why hasn't the Disney Company made a sequel to *Bambi?*

It would be a stag movie.

———————

Why did so many people want to add Ronald Reagan to Mount Rushmore?

His head was already the right size.

———————

Did you hear that Lassie went to Denmark?

She came back a cat.

———————

What do Donald Trump's children do at Christmastime?

Sit on Santa's lap and ask him what he needs.

What happened to the hooker who worked the steps of the Capitol?

She was subjected to several congressional probes.

_____

Why was Ted Bundy's mother so disappointed in him?

He never dated the same girl twice.

_____

What did Dan Quayle do when Bush ordered him to tour Central America?

He made reservations to visit Illinois, Kansas, and Iowa.

_____

Why did Dan Quayle sign up for Latin lessons?

President Bush sent him to Latin America.

The Lone Ranger and his faithful friend Tonto rode up onto the crest of a hill. Suddenly, the masked man signaled a stop. "Tonto, there's a war party of Apaches in front of us."

"Let's go east," Tonto said.

"There's a tribe of Sioux camping on the plain."

"Well, Kemo Sabe, we go west."

"There's Pawnees to the west. And that band of Blackfeet are closing behind us to the south. Tonto, how will we escape?"

Tonto looked at him and said, "What do you mean, 'we,' white man?"

———————

How bad is the crisis in the savings and loan industry?

So bad that twenty-two congressmen have declared bankruptcy.

———————

Why was Ted Bundy like a bad golfer?

He always took a few slices before he put it in the hole.

How can you make a Lebanese tourist feel at home?

Bomb his hotel room.

———————

Why don't terrorists ever attack a Northwest Airlines flight?

By takeoff, the pilots are already bombed.

———————

Why didn't Dan Quayle fly to Colombia with the President on Air Force One?

He forgot the flight number.

———————

Why is pregnancy so magical in Hollywood?

The minute a starlet knows she's pregnant, the father disappears.

What's Iran?

The one country in the world where a man can really talk his head off.

———————————

Who's the most frequent traveler in the Bush administration?

Vice President Quayle. Even when he's in his office, his mind is wandering.

Chapter Three

Gross Animal Jokes

How can you tell if a termite is gay?

He'll only eat woodpeckers.

_____

Did you hear about the new Australian porno film?

Sheep Throat.

Why do frogs have the worst sex life in the animal kingdom?

They hop on, hop off, then croak.

_____

How can you tell if a canine is a fire dog?

He locates hydrants.

_____

Why is a pair of rabbits the perfect gift for the person who has everything?

It's a gift that keeps on giving.

_____

How do you teach a dog to fetch?

Tie a cat to a stick.

The couple were called in to see the school psychologist. "Little Johnny is a terrific kid," the husband said. "I don't understand why we're here."

"You're here because your son has been taking in stray cats," the school psychologist said.

"See, that proves he's terrific," the wife said.

"I don't think so," the psychologist replied. "He's been feeding them to stray dogs."

———————

Where do you go to buy a dog?

A used cur dealer.

———————

A woman was walking her German shepherd in the park one day when a guy came up and said, "Excuse me, but I was wondering one thing. Isn't it dangerous to have a savage animal like that around the house?"

"Nonsense," the woman replied. "Trojan is a perfect gentleman. He never growls, never barks. He's kind to children, polite with strangers, and what's more, even loves a little pussy."

"That's interesting," the man said. "You mean he actually lives in the same house as a cat?"

"I never said I owned a cat," the woman said.

Why did the Polack feed nylon to his chickens?

He wanted them to lay L'Eggs.

_____

Why shouldn't you screw chickens?

The cops consider it fowl play.

_____

What would you get if you crossed a chicken with your husband?

A cock that couldn't get up in the morning.

_____

What do you call it when a porcupine's ready for sex?

Prickly heat.

What do you call a rabbit with herpes?

Peter Rotten Tail.

What do you call a rabbit with crabs?

Bugs Bunny.

What happens when your rabbit gets AIDS?

You lose your hare.

Did you hear about the poverty-stricken snake?

He didn't have a pit to hiss in.

It was time for the annual Army war games, and the men of the 2nd Platoon, 3rd Company, 18th Infantry were assigned to set an ambush for the enemy. For weeks, the soldiers worked to camouflage themselves as trees. Finally, the big day came and the platoon took their places.

The brigade commander watched as the enemy approached the ambush. But just before the trap was to be sprung, one private suddenly jumped in the air and dashed away. Furious, the general ordered the man to be brought to him, then said, "Soldier, you're going to be court-martialed for disobeying orders. How could you move?"

"Well, sir," the private replied. "It was this way. I didn't even think about moving when the birds landed on my branches and shit all over me. I didn't move when the dog came by and peed on my legs. I didn't budge when a squirrel climbed up each leg. Then I heard one squirrel say to the other, 'Let's eat one now and bury the other one for winter.'"

Chapter Four

Gross Homosexual Jokes

Why is a San Francisco hair dresser like a bee?

At the end of every day, he goes home to a queen.

———————————

A very swishy young man from the country thought he'd died and gone to heaven when his equally queer cousin showed him around San Francisco. By the time they entered a gay bar, the country faggot was so excited that he approached the first guy at the bar, dropped to his knees, pulled down his zipper, and went to work. A few minutes later he moved to the next guy, then the next, then the next.

Finally, his cousin came over and said, "Brucie, do you want to leave?"

"No way," he replied as he pulled down yet another zipper. "Time is sure fun when you're having flies."

Why do so many fags work as theater ushers?

Every guy who walks in has to flash his stub.

How do we know all feminists are lesbians?

They want all women of the world to unite.

How can fags keep humping each other all night long?

Every fairy has a magic wand.

What's a transvestite's favorite sport?

Drag racing.

––––––––––––––––––

A couple was expecting their first child. He wanted a boy, and she wanted a girl.

Then Bruce was born, and they both got their wish.

––––––––––––––––––

How can you tell a gay brothel?

The entrance is in the rear.

––––––––––––––––––

What's a fag's favorite candy?

Cum suckers.

How do you recognize the gay criminal?

He's the one mugging the florist.

What's another name for fags with AIDS?

Tool and die workers.

What's worse than getting kissed by a fag with AIDS?

Getting a hickey from a cannibal.

Why is homosexuality like cigarette smoking?

Either way, too many butts can kill you.

What do you call fag shit?

Toxic waste.

Where does it come from?

Their Love Canal.

_____

What do you call diaphragms for gays?

Fruit loops.

_____

Why do gays love paper salesmen?

Paper salesmen are always good for a ream or two.

_____

"How's your love life?" one woman asked another.

"Well, I've met this guy," the second woman said.
"He's a lawyer, he's about six two with blue eyes, he's got
a gorgeous build, he doesn't smoke, doesn't drink,
doesn't do drugs, and he's always been totally honest and

forthright with me."

"Wow!" the first woman exclaimed. "That's great. What else should I know about him?"

The second woman grimaced. "He also makes all his own dresses."

———————————

Who are the most fiscally responsible people?

Homosexuals—they always make ends meet.

———————————

The big, mean, ugly biker had a reputation for gay-bashing, so the cops picked him up after a few faggots had disappeared. They took the biker into a room and asked, "We know you don't have a job, asshole. So what do you do with your time?"

The guy sneered, "You might say I'm into gardening."

"Gardening?"

"Yeah," the biker replied. "There's nothing I like better than planting pansies."

What do congressmen do in their spare time?

Many like a good book, while a few are satisfied by a single page.

Chapter Five

A Gross Variety

Did you hear about the guy who held up a lawyer's office?

He lost $1100.

––––––––––––––

Why don't cannibals eat missionaries?

You can't keep a good man down.

Did you hear about the JAP leper?

She talked her head off.

_____

Why did the cannibal put the faggot in the food processor?

He wanted fruit salad.

_____

What happened to the leper who walked into a screen door?

He strained himself.

_____

Did you hear about the lazy cannibal?

He's been living off his family for a year.

A man came home from work one night and his wife said, "Harry, I really don't like that sex-education class Christopher's attending at school."

"Don't be a prude, Doris," the husband said. "Chris has got to learn about the birds and the bees."

"It isn't what they're learning in class that bothers me."

"Then what is it?"

"Today, he came home and told me he needed $50 for a field trip," Doris replied.

The family was sitting at the dinner table when six-year-old Jamie asked, "Daddy, why is Miss Jenkins next door giving you clothes?"

The mother flashed the father a dirty look and said, "Is that true, Henry?"

"Of course that isn't true," the father hurriedly replied. "Why would she give me clothes?"

"I don't know," the lad replied. "But I heard her talking on the phone to somebody and she said she was giving you a paternity suit."

The third-grade class at Our Lady of the Precious Blood parochial school was preparing for a visit by the archbishop. For weeks, the class was drilled by a stern Sister Mary Joseph to answer a series of questions about the Bible.

Finally, the big day arrived. The archbishop was ushered to a seat in the classroom, and a dozen boys and girls stood stiffly in front of him. As the principal asked the questions, Sister Mary Joseph stood right behind the student, giving him or her a jab in the ribs with her pointer to jar the memory.

The last boy in line was little Tommy. "What did Eve say to Adam?" the principal asked. Tommy hesitated, and Sister let him have it. Immediately, the boy said, "Hey, don't stick that thing in me!"

Then the archbishop turned red, got up, and left the room.

The sixth-grade teacher was conducting a class on careers. She pointed to little Teddy and said, "Tell us what you want to do when you grow up and why you want to do it."

"I'm going to be a doctor," Teddy said, "so I can spend my days making sick people well."

"Very good," the teacher said. She pointed to a little girl and said, "Sarah, tell us what you want to do when you grow up and why?"

"I want to be a piano teacher," Sarah replied, "so I can spend my days helping people make beautiful music."

"Excellent," the teacher said. She pointed to a boy in the corner and said, "Joey, what do you want to be when you grow up?"

Joey thought for a moment, then said, "I want to be just like Colonel Sanders."

The teacher looked puzzled. "Why in heaven's name would you like to be like Colonel Sanders?"

"Because," Joey replied, "I want to spend my days looking at naked legs and breasts."

———————————

What's different about flying on a cannibal airline?

Your luggage gets the seat, while you ride in the belly.

———————————

Why are plastic surgeons like the U.S. State Department?

They both specialize in aid to underdeveloped areas.

What are the two best reasons for becoming a teacher?

July and August.

Did you hear that researchers have pinpointed the cause of teenage pregnancy?

It's called a "date."

What happened to the cannibal who moved to Poland?

He looked around, then became a vegetarian.

How can you tell a WASP kid?

He's the one who asks for his allowance in yen.

A little girl was sitting in the living room sobbing her eyes out when her mother asked, "Darling, what's wrong?"

"I want to have a pet."

"Now, dear," her mother said, "you know I'm allergic to fur. We can't have a pet."

"Oh, yeah!" the little girl said. "Then how come the maid can have a pet."

"What makes you think Maria has a pet?"

"Last night I heard Daddy tell her he loved her pussy."

———————

The father spent almost every minute of his spare time sitting in the family room watching sports and drinking beer. That's why the mother was astounded one Saturday when she came home and heard her little boy say, "Mommy, Mommy, Daddy took me to the zoo today."

"I don't believe it," the mother said.

"Yeah," the little lad said. "And guess what—one of the animals paid $30!"

———————

A high school senior turned to his friend and said, "I don't understand girls. Last night, Margie was so friendly that I screwed her three times in the back seat of my Volkswagen. This morning, she won't talk to me."

"She must be sore," the friend replied.

A WASP mother, a Jewish mother, and an Italian mother were talking in the doctor's office. "My son Winston has been accepted by a very elite prep school," the WASP mother bragged. "You need a recommendation from a congressman to get in."

"My Sydney has just been accepted by the finest Hebrew school in the country," the Jewish mother said. "You have to be recommended by a rabbi to get in."

"My Tony just started a special school, too," the Italian mother said. "You have to be sent there by a judge."

Two kids were in their playroom when one said to the other, "Let's play doctor."

"All right," the other said. "We'll take turns. First you operate, and I'll sue."

Did you hear about the cannibal couple who committed suicide?

She joined him in a bowl of soup.

Why do cannibal wives try to stay drab and dumpy?

The last thing they want is for their husbands to approach them with relish.

––––––––––––

The most festive occasion in the cannibal world was coming up, and the tribe members went far and wide to collect food for the big event. One group captured a couple of missionaries, another nabbed some big game hunters, and third came back with a tour bus. All the captives were held in a holding pen for days. Finally, the very nervous white men were amazed to see a small plane land next to the remote village. The cannibals dragged a very strange-looking group of people out of the plane. Puzzled, one of the captives asked, "What's that all about?"

"Oh, we sent a plane to London to grab some patients from a mental institution," a cannibal said.

"Why?"

"Because," the cannibal replied, "for special occasions, we want everything from soup to nuts."

––––––––––––

What do cannibals serve at formal teas?

Ladyfingers.

What's a sex pot?

It's where a cannibal cooks a hooker.

What's a cannibal's favorite food?

Old men—their meat's always tender.

An American was traveling in rural China when he developed an excruciating toothache. He managed to travel to a village, where he was escorted to the local dentist. Through his interpreter, he asked, "How much is it to remove a tooth?"

The interpreter consulted the dentist, then told him, "He say $1,000 U.S. money. They have to take the tooth out through your nose."

The American's aching jaw dropped. "That's ridiculous. Why through my nose?"

The interpreter relayed the comment to the dentist, who replied, "That's the only way he knows. In China, people not allowed to open mouth."

What's a cannibal boxer's favorite food?

Knuckle sandwiches.

———————

Two cannibals had been to a baseball game that afternoon, and at dinner one said to the other, "What do you think of that new right fielder?"

"I'm not sure he's a star," the second cannibal said, "but," he added, taking a big bite, "he does have a terrific arm."

Chapter Six

Gross Religious Jokes

Why do priests masturbate?

"God helps those who help themselves."

———————————

Why did the Polish girl think she was Jesus Christ?

She got nailed three times on Good Friday.

The minister was standing at the door of the church after the service when a man came up, shook his hand, and said, "Let me tell you, Reverend, that was one hell of a sermon you gave today."

"Thank you for the compliment, sir," the clergyman replied, "but I must caution you that the Lord forbids profanity."

"Sorry," the man said. "I guess I got carried away. I was so impressed I dropped $500 in the collection plate."

The minister's jaw dropped. "No shit!"

———————————

The Mother Superior had been a true and devoted servant of the Blessed Virgin for all of her eighty-four years. Finally, she passed away and soon after stood before the Pearly Gates. Saint Peter greeted her with deference and escorted her to an audience with Virgin Mary herself. The Mother Superior fell to her knees and expressed her adulation. The Blessed Virgin graciously told her to rise.

The old nun obeyed, then said, "I so love and admire you. It must be a thrill beyond human imagination to have given birth to the Saviour of mankind."

The Virgin Mary shrugged. "To be honest, I wanted he should be a doctor."

An Italian guy walks up to the door of the whorehouse one Saturday night and rings the bell. When the madam opens it, the guy says, "Let me in. I gotta get laid."

"Sorry," she says. "We're all full up. Come back tomorrow."

The guy is crushed. But as he starts to walk away, he gets an idea. He goes back to the door, knocks, then tells the madam, "You want to have some fun? Just let me in and I'll whisper to one of the guys inside that the nuns at the convent down the block all got drunk and are giving away pussy. I guarantee you they'll all forget they've paid and rush out. That'll leave room for me."

The madam smiled, then let him in. The wop whispered to the first guy he saw. Sure enough, within ten minutes there was a stampede to the door. The madam was roaring at the foolishness when, to her surprise, she saw the Italian guy leaving with the rest. She grabbed him and said, "Where are you going?"

The guy shrugged and said, "With all these guys leaving, maybe there's something to it after all."

———————————

The rabbi was facing a family crisis, so in desperation he went off into the desert to fast and pray. For day after day, he endured the blazing sun and frigid nights until finally, the Lord appeared unto him.

"Why dost thou beseech me?" The Lord asked.

"My only son is about to become a Christian," the rabbi said.

God grimaced. "Your son!"

Where does a rabbi keep all his clippings?

In his tool box.

Why should priests be allowed to marry?

Then they'd know what hell is really like.

Why is religion like golf?

A lot of people practice, but very few are good at it.

All the nuns in the convent spent the entire day in church praying. After hours on her knees, one nun finally fainted and keeled over. A young novice gasped in surprise, but the Mother Superior said, "Don't worry, my dear. We have a remedy that has been used in this convent for centuries." She opened a black case, took out a large bottle of brandy, and added, "We keep this for medicinal purposes only."

The Mother Superior then went over to the fallen nun,

shook her until she regained consciousness, then gave her a hefty swig of the strong liquor. Immediately, the color returned to the nun's face and she resumed praying.

About half an hour later, another nun keeled over. Once again, Mother Superior reached into her black case, got the bottle, and administered a dose. The young novice watched, but didn't say anything.

By the end of the day, almost every nun had fainted. The young novice, who had totally committed herself to the service of the Lord, was increasingly repulsed by the strong odor of liquor and by the idea of serving it in God's house. As the Mother Superior administered the medicine once again, the novice said, "Mother Superior, in this age of medical miracles, there is surely a better remedy for fainting."

"Maybe," the head nun replied, "but in all my years, no one's asked."

_____

The little five-year-old Italian boy had seldom ventured outside his community until his parents rented a vacation cabin on a mountain lake. Upon their arrival, they discovered that a family of WASPs had rented the cabin next to them. For a day or two the Italians kept to themselves. But finally, the little boy went to his parents and asked, "Mama, Papa, I got nothing to do. Can I play with that little girl next door?"

The parents reluctantly gave their permission. But the mother said, "Now, don't you go getting too friendly.

We're Catholics and they're Protestants."

"What does that mean?" the little boy asked.

"That means we're different," the mother replied.

Satisfied, the boy scampered off and soon made a new friend. A couple of days later, the two tots were down by the lake when they decided to wade into the water. The boy stripped off his clothes, turned to the naked girl, looked between her legs, and gasped, "Boy, you Protestants sure are different!"

A Baptist minister was walking down the street with some older members of his congregation when he saw a gorgeous black hooker in hot pants soliciting customers on the corner. Anxious to impress his flock, the minister went up to her and said, "Sister, it is time for you to repent and banish Satan from your heart."

"Don't talk that shit at me, Reverend," the hooker retorted. "I can take those folks over there closer to heaven than you can."

"You blasphemer!" the minister blustered. "When Judgment Day comes, Jesus will punish you."

"Jesus, shit," the hooker said. "If that Jesus had been with me, he wouldn't have the strength for no Second Coming."

A very naive young man found himself getting very nervous and tense around girls, so he went to see his minister to get some advice. When he got to the parsonage, however, the very shapely young secretary told him the minister had been called away to visit a sick parishioner. The young man got to talking to the girl about his problem. Finally she said, "I think I may be able to do something about that."

She led him into the minister's living quarters, found a bed, and proceeded to initiate him into the wonders of sex. When they were done, the young man said, "Is there any way I can thank you?"

"Well, you can make a $25 donation," the girl said. The young man forked over the money and left.

A couple of weeks later, he started feeling nervous and tense again, so he made another journey to the parsonage. This time the minister was in. He listened to the young man's story, counseled him to turn to prayer when he felt the need, and added, "It would also serve the Lord and your needs if you saw fit to make a $10 donation to the church."

"If it's all the same to you," the young man replied, "I'd rather qualify for the $25 donation."

———————————

The parish priest dropped into a local bar one evening to wet his whistle. As he took a seat, he looked over to see a very buxom redhead whose massive jugs nearly burst out of a low-cut, skintight dress. The priest stared intently for a couple of minutes until he heard the bartender say, "Father McReynolds, you should be ashamed of yourself."

Red-faced, the priest stammered, "Oh, I wasn't staring at her. I . . . I thought it was the daughter of a parishioner. Now, please, go get me a nice piece of beer."

———————

Did you hear about the homosexual priest?

After every Mass, he felt like a new man.

———————

Did you hear about the priest who gave up drinking?

It was the longest twenty minutes of his life.

———————

Two nuns were walking home late one night after bingo when they noticed three soldiers following them down a dark street. One nun turned nervously to the other and asked, "Aren't those soldiers out after hours?"

"I hope so," the other nun replied eagerly.

After Mass, the altar boy said, "Father, I have to talk to you. Since I turned thirteen, I keep getting erections. I know touching myself is a sin, but the urge is so strong. Please help me with this problem."

So the priest said, "Of course I will, my son," then licked it for him.

A priest and a nun were driving back to their parish from a meeting when they skidded off the deserted snowy road into a ditch. With no way to move the car, the two faced a night alone.

"What should we do, Father?" the young nun asked fearfully.

"Don't worry, my child," the priest said. "Let us huddle together for warmth, pray, and the Lord will bless us."

The two huddled together. And by the time dawn came, the priest had experienced a piece no man had ever had before.

Did you hear about the group of homosexual priests?

They organized a retreat so they could make some advances.

Chapter Seven

Gross Jokes About Senior Citizens

Why is sex with an eighty-year-old man like complaining to the IRS?

In either case, you get no response.

What's an old maid's birthday cake?

You put batter in a pan, stick in candles, light them, and the cake bakes itself.

How do you know you're getting old?

The only time you breathe heavily at night is when you walk up a flight of stairs.

––––––––––––––

A woman was out antiquing with her mother. She walked into one shop, pulled out an old, dusty metal object, and asked, "What is this?"

"Madam, that's an antique bedwarmer," the shop owner replied. "It is priced at $350."

"Hell," the woman's mother snorted, "I've got one of those. And I'll lend him to you for $10."

––––––––––––––

The doctor walked into the hospital room of an eighty-six-year-old man and said, "Mr. Reynolds, I have some good news and some bad news."

The old man said, "Well, Son, tell me the good news first."

The doctor replied, "The good news is that your condition could be completely corrected by a transplant. The bad news is that they no longer make the parts."

What's the definition of embarrassment?

Two thirty-nine-year-old women meeting in the Social Security office.

_____

What's the difference between middle age and old age?

In middle age, you flip on a porno movie before you hop in bed with your wife; in old age, you call Dial-A-Prayer.

_____

Why did the old maid buy two candles?

In case she wanted to light one.

_____

Why is it cruel to make old people give up smoking?

Coughing and wheezing's the only exercise they get.

How did the old woman know she'd had too many face-lifts?

When she raised her eyebrows, her stockings tore.

How do you know you're getting old?

If you tell your buddy you spent the day with a hooker, he knows you've been playing golf.

Exactly how ugly was the old maid?

She couldn't even get a date on her tombstone.

What's middle age?

It's when a guy moves from hardball to softball.

Two old black women were sitting in church one day after services when one said to the other, "It's gettin' to be the time when I meet my maker. I sure does hopes he forgives my youth and sends me to heaven with my children."

The other old black woman nods in agreement. "I wants to go to glory myself. But if I has to go to hell, I want to go where that landlord of mine be sent."

"You hate that old Jew," the first woman said. "Why you want to go to hell with him?"

"Because," the other replied, "I knows for sure that wherever Shapiro is, the heat won't work."

The old man and the old woman had remained married for fifty-seven years, even though he was the stingiest person in the entire world. Finally, the long suffering wife was on her deathbed. A single candle flickered by her bedside as she said, "I'm so weak. I don't think I'll be here in the morning."

Her husband rose to go downstairs, then said, "I hope you feel better. But if you should feel yourself dying, make sure to blow that candle out."

After Milton retired, he spent every waking minute following sports. He pored over the sports pages every morning, subscribed to a dozen sports magazines, and spent at least a dozen hours a day switching channels from event to event. At first, his wife was glad that he was busy, but she soon came to hate how sports dominated every moment of his time.

One night, as he was lying next to her in bed watching a baseball game, she got up, walked across the room, and unplugged the TV set.

"Hey," he shouted. "What do you think you're doing?"

"Milton," she replied, "I'm sick of sports. You haven't touched me in weeks. I insist that we talk about sex."

"All right," Milton agreed. "I'll start. How often do you think Darryl Strawberry gets laid?"

The seventy-eight-year-old man took a twenty-two-year-old bride. A few weeks later, he went to see his doctor, who asked, "How are things going with your young bride?"

"Pretty well," the old man said. "The only thing that bothers me is that she always wants to make love in the backseat of the car."

"Uncomfortable, huh?" the doctor said.

"It's not that," the old man said. "It's that she insists that I drive."

Fred met his usually dour friend Harry at the senior citizen center. To Fred's surprise, Harry had a big grin on his face. "What happened?" Fred asked. "Did that battleax wife of yours finally pass away?"

"I'm not that lucky," the other man replied. "But she did finally get a job at the drugstore that gets her out of the house all day."

"The drugstore?" Fred said. "You mean she's a cashier?"

"No," Harry replied. "It's a better job than that. She stands around outside and makes people sick."

Why don't old women wear belts?

They can't tighten them because their tits get in the way.

How ugly was the old maid?

She had to blindfold herself when she took a bath.

A terrible storm had ravaged the Maine coast for two days. When the weather finally passed, a lobsterman preparing his boat for sea got a call from the Coast Guard.

"I've got some terrible news for you," the captain said. "One of our cutters found the body of your mother floating in the bay with two lobsters latched on to her toes and two on to her fingers. What do you want us to do?"

"Hold the lobsters so I can sell them," the lobsterman replied. "And set her body out in the bay again."

Chapter Eight

Gross Sex Jokes

How do you know a guy is a loser?

The only way he can see a female figure naked is to buy the clothes off a department store dummy.

———————

How can you tell a guy is a real loser?

He only wakes up stiff if he jogged ten miles the night before.

One guy was sitting at the bar when his buddy asked, "Hey, Fred. What would you do if you came home and found a guy humping your wife?"

"I'd be pissed," Fred replied. "I'd break his white cane, shoot his dog, and then call the loony bin he escaped from."

———————

Why can't a man eat like a bird?

You ever try picking up food with your pecker?

———————

What's a "quack"?

A perfect pwace to put a pwick.

———————

What's the ideal male birth-control pill?

One that changes your blood type.

What's the lightest object in the world?

A penis. Even a thought can raise it.

———————————

A guy was sitting on the train looking glum when a friend asked, "What's wrong, Charlie?"

"It's my wife," the guy replied. "She's threatening to divorce me because we have communication problems."

"You don't talk to her?"

"I talk to her all time," the guy complained. "She's mad because I won't tell her who I'm dating."

———————————

Why are women so bad in math?

Because they've spent their whole lives being told that this (hold two fingers up a couple of inches apart) is eight inches.

———————————

What's the best way to get an ugly girl to give you head?

Dip your cock in Gravy Train.

What's the best way to get an ugly girl to give you a hand job?

Put a Milk Bone in your fly.

How do you know you've got a really small dick?

You flash a policewoman and you're arrested for carrying a concealed weapon.

A guy was sitting at the bar looking glum when a buddy asked, "What's wrong, Jim?"

"It's this girl I'm dating."

"Won't put out, huh?"

"That's not it," Jim said. "She's terrific in bed. She's a great cook. And she makes twice as much money as I do. The only problem is, she agrees with everything I say."

"That's a problem?" the buddy asked incredulously.

"Yeah. That means she could be lying about everything else, too."

Why are women more careful drivers than men?

If they have an accident, the newspaper prints their ages.

_____

Why is sex hereditary?

If your parents never had it, you never will.

_____

Why do most women look gross in tight pants?

Their ends don't justify the jeans.

_____

Why is a topless bar like a sculpture garden?

The purpose of both is to unveil a few busts.

A woman was talking to a friend at lunch when she said, "I've been having terrible headaches, and the doctor hasn't helped me at all."

"Why don't you try acupuncture?" the friend said.

"Do you think it really works?"

"Think about how much better you feel after you've had just one prick," the friend replied.

What was the very first male putdown?

Eve walked into the Garden of Eden, glanced at Adam, and said, "You could get by with a smaller fig leaf."

Why did the woman call her husband's dick "Miller Lite"?

It tasted good, but it wasn't very filling.

Why is a penis like a newborn baby?

They both get bigger from sucking.

Why don't masturbators ever panic?

They always have a firm grip on themselves.

––––––––––––––

A guy was sitting at the bar when a friend said, "Hey, Joe. I heard you got a new girlfriend. What's she like?"

"Well, she's one of those Venus de Milo broads," Joe replied.

"What do you mean?"

"She's beautiful, but she's not all there."

––––––––––––––

What's bigamy?

It's where two rites make a wrong.

––––––––––––––

Why do women like their nipples licked?

It brings out their best points.

Why did the girl slap her boyfriend?

She didn't like the way he was feeling about her.

———————————

Why is the post office like a frustrated wife?

They're both looking for ways to slow down the male.

———————————

What kind of pet does a Peeping Tom own?

A watch dog.

———————————

What makes a nymphomaniac so tired?

Working her fingers to your bone.

What's an X-rated movie?

A boy meats girl story.

———————

What do you call it when a nymphomaniac talks about her dates?

An organ recital.

———————

What's the ideal husband?

A guy with a million-dollar life insurance policy who dies on your wedding day.

———————

Two women were sitting at a bar when a guy walked in. One said to the other, "That guy looks kind of cute."

The second woman grimaced. "He's a loser. All he likes is cafeteria sex."

"What's cafeteria sex?"

"Self-service only," the second woman replied.

Why isn't wife-swapping a good idea?

It's so depressing when you get your wife back.

———————————

What do you call a man who has an angel for a wife?

A widower.

———————————

How do we know that sex can cause loss of memory?

Ask your husband where he was until two A.M. last night.

———————————

How can you tell when a guy likes food more than sex?

He installs a mirror over his kitchen table.

A WASP, a black guy, and a Polack were sitting in a bar drinking when the WASP said, "I'm very proud of my girlfriend. She called me last night and announced she won the tennis championship at the club."

"That's nothing, man," the black dude said. "My chick called last night and told me she set a new state record in the hundred-meter dash."

"That's nothing," the Polack added, "compared to my girlfriend."

"I've seen your girlfriend try to bowl," the WASP said. "She can't walk and chew gum at the same time."

"Oh, yeah," the Polack retorted. "Well, she came home from the bar late last night and told me she made the basketball team."

———————————

Why do women love race car drivers?

They take lots of pit stops between laps.

———————————

Did you hear about the X-rated murder mystery?

In the end, everyone did it.

A guy was in bed with his neighbor's wife when he heard the door slam downstairs. Panicked, he jumped out of bed and climbed out the window. Unfortunately, the husband was waiting for him in the garden with a shotgun in hand. Before the guy could say a word the husband pulled the trigger, sending a load of pellets into his groin.

A couple of days later, the guy woke up in a hospital bed. He looked up and saw a woman standing over him. Groggily, he asked, "Are you my nurse?"

"No," she replied. "I'm a flute teacher."

"Listen, lady," the guy snapped. "I've just been shot. I don't need a flute teacher."

"Oh, yeah?" she replied. Pointing to his bandaged cock, she added, "How else do you think you're going to learn how to pee with that thing?"

Why is buying a used car like going to a brothel?

You're a hundred percent sure you're going to get screwed.

Why are professional golfers such lousy lovers?

Four strokes, and they're on to the next hole.

How did the U.S. government take the fun out of wife-swapping?

It passed the truth-in-lending law.

———————————

What happened when the brothel went on strike?

Everything came to a grinding halt.

———————————

How do you know a guy is a loser?

He tries to buy a ticket to a porno movie, and the cashier tells him she's got a headache.

———————————

How do you know a girl is flat-chested?

She needs suspenders to hold up her bra.

How do you know a girl is flat-chested?

She lies down in the garden, rubs honey on her nipples, and prays for bees.

What's puberty?

The age when a Boy Scout becomes a girl scout.

Why is it risky to open a sperm bank?

Your business comes in spurts.

J. Barensfeld Tipton III, the very snotty, spoiled scion of one of America's wealthiest families, was finally getting married. The day before the big event, he was sitting on the veranda of the Tipton estate with his parents, inspecting some wedding gifts.

"Look, darling," his mother said. "Aunt Celia bought you a new Rolls."

The young man strolled around the car, made an

unpleasant face, and said, "Tell Jeeves to return it. There is a speck of dust on the rear fender."

"Don't be ridiculous," his mother scolded. "You don't throw away a $200,000 car because of a speck of dust. Jeeves will see that it is removed."

A few minutes later, a servant approached leading a magnificent stallion. "You are very fortunate, J.B.," his father advised. "Your uncle Oswald has purchased last year's Grand National champion for you."

The young man strolled around the stallion, made an unpleasant face, and said, "Have the horse returned. I saw a tangle on the left side of its mane."

"That's foolish," his father scolded. "You don't throw away a million-dollar horse because a groom made a small mistake. The groom will recomb the mane."

The disgruntled bridegroom stalked away. The next day, a thousand guests arrived for young Tipton's marriage to the ravishingly beautiful, incredibly wealthy blond bride. Finally, the guests left, the newlyweds retreated to the honeymoon cottage on the estate, and the elder Tiptons started to relax. Then, to their shock, their son burst into the room and said, "The marriage is off. Send her back to her family."

The father stammered, "But, Son . . ."

"And don't tell me I'm throwing away a $50 million dollar dowry for nothing," the outraged prig replied. "Why, when that girl took off her clothes, I could see right away there was a big hole in her!"

The building had once been a fast-food restaurant, so the madam kept the same motif when she turned it into a whorehouse. On opening day, a customer came in the door and the madam handed him a menu. "Would you like some suggestions?" she asked.

"Sure," the john replied.

"Well," the madam said, "you may enjoy the 'Burger King.'"

"What's that?"

"You have it your way," the madam replied.

"Sounds good," said the john. He read a little further, then asked, "What's a 'Colonel Sanders'?"

"When you buy a piece, you get a choice between regular and extra horny," the madam said.

"That's interesting," the john replied. He read further, then asked, "What's the 'Pizza Hut'?"

"You can eat two pieces for the price of one."

"That's for me," the guy said. The madam called in his order, and soon two luscious naked Italian girls were delivered to his room. When the madam left, he appeared to be in seventh heaven as he dove for their bushes. However, a couple of minutes later, he stormed out of the room and approached the madam.

"Is there something wrong?" she asked.

"Yeah," he said. "I forgot to tell you to hold the anchovies."

The foursome had just teed off on the tenth hole when an assistant pro came running up to Mr. Dobkin and said, "I'm very sorry to have to tell you this, sir. But we just received word that your wife has been killed in an automobile accident."

Dobkin turned to his companions and said, "Fellows, I have to warn you. As soon as we finish the eighteenth hole, you're going to see a man cry his heart out."

How do you know a guy has an ugly wife?

His pet name for her is "Rover".

Did you hear about the small-town hooker who chewed tobacco all day?

They sent her to jail after twenty-three men died of cancer of the penis.

How do you know if your wife's cooking is really bad?

Natives come from the Amazon to dip their arrows in it.

_____

Why are women such an enigma?

Most of them have to get tight before they're loose.

_____

Two guys were sitting at the bar when one said to the other, "How's that dentist friend of yours doing?"

The second guy grimaced. "His wife's suing him for divorce because of a root canal."

"A root canal? How can she be mad about what he did to some patient?"

"Because she walked in and saw his root in her canal."

_____

A hooker moved into the small town and began working out of a trailer. It had been a long time since the world's oldest profession had been practiced in the town, so a line of men formed outside the trailer. Seeing the line, the hooker came out and announced, "I want to move right along here. Get out your wallets and unbuckle your belts. You get ten minutes for $20."

The first guy who walked in was so excited that he finished in a couple of minutes. But the timer went off while the next guy was pumping away. When the hooker pushed him off, the guy protested, "I haven't even come yet."

The hooker shrugged and said, "I'm running this business and your time is up. You'll have to come back again."

"Well, me and most of those guys outside work in the bottling plant," the guy said. "And you know what we say in that business?"

"What?"

"No deposit, no return."

What's a rapist?

A stick-up artist.

What's better than a wife who's made to order?

A ready maid.

Why shouldn't you worry when people brag about their family trees?

Because in reality, everybody pops out of a bush.

———————————

Why is it a pain to have a nymphomaniac for Thanksgiving dinner?

She always wants more stuffing.

———————————

How can you tell your marriage might not be a good idea?

Your wife has male bridesmaids.

———————————

One of the twin teenage sisters came home from a date with a big grin on her face. "What happened?" her sister asked.

The other twin said, "Guess what? We're not identical anymore."

Two guys were sitting at a bar talking about their wives. "My old lady is so ugly," one said, "that the beauty parlor told her there was nothing more they could do."

"You think that's bad? I took my wife to a plastic surgeon and asked him what he could do to make her look better. The only thing he could think of was adding a tail."

———————

A woman walked into the furniture store and said, "I'm interested in a sexual sofa."

The salesman blushed, then said, "Miss, I think you mean sectional sofa."

"Nah," the woman said. "I know what I want. My boyfriend wants an occasional piece in the living room."

———————

Why is prostitution recession-proof?

Hookers thrive on hard times.

How do we know women are dynamite?

Try dropping one.

———————————

How can you tell if a streetwalker is Polish?

She thinks the customers are the ones driving around with the red light on top of the car.

———————————

The very pregnant Hollywood starlet was sitting in the doctor's waiting room staring intently at the wall. The nurse called her name three times, then had to touch her to get her attention. "Wow," the nurse said, "you were really lost in thought."

"I was thinking about a name," the starlet said.
"For the baby?"
"No. For the paternity suit."

A guy walked into a bar and ordered a triple Scotch on the rocks. When the bartender walked over, he noticed the guy had a huge shiner around his left eye. "What happened to you, George?" he asked.

The guy grimaced. "Well, I told you before that I've been after my wife for years to give me a blow job. Finally, she told me that she'd go down on me if I came home with something for her to drive."

"So what happened?"

"I told her I would. So I got my blow job and I came home tonight with a golf ball."

———————

About sixty percent of the females in this country are working women.

The rest are working men.

———————

If you get leather from tanning cow's hide and feathers from plucking a bird, how do you get a mink coat?

By skinning your husband.

Why is a ladies' man like a theater critic?

He spends every night at a new opening.

How can you tell a guy is a loser?

When a girl tells him she's horny, he rubs her head.

A guy was sitting at the bar when he said to his friend, "I think Harriet is really angry that we're going hunting this weekend."

"How can you tell?"

"When I came home last night, I found out she'd bought me a deerskin coat."

A businessman was meeting with a co-worker. He pushed a button and asked his secretary to come in with coffee and the Rushington report.

A couple of minutes later, this well-built redhead walked in, tripped over her high heels, and spilled coffee over both men. As she attempted to mop up the mess, she knocked over a lamp. When that mess was cleaned up, she handed the co-worker a report that had every other word crossed out or misspelled.

The guy turned to the businessman and said, "How did you ever come to hire her?"

"I knew she was the perfect person for the job when I asked her what her last position was."

"What did she say?"

"She said it was 'doggie style.'"

Two businessmen were sitting at lunch when one said, "I had to fire my secretary this morning. She came in two hours late."

"This morning I had to give my secretary a big raise because she came in late," the other said.

"Why did you give her money for being late?"

"She was two months late," the second businessman replied.

Two coeds were sitting in the cafeteria when one said to another, "I can't believe my luck. Every time I go out on a date, I spend the rest of the evening fighting off the guy's attacks."

"So what are you going to do?" her friend asked.

"Date stronger guys," she replied.

Why did the bank manager take the luscious blond teller into the vault?

For safe sex.

_____

What do you call it when nymphomaniacs get together for drinks?

Cock-tale hour.

_____

Why should you take your wedding vows seriously?

You'll never get on'er if you don't obey.

_____

Why is safe sex like baseball?

If you want to pitch, you need a rubber.

Why is furniture like sex?

It's best when there's a great finish.

In this populated country, what's rarer than a virgin forest?

A virgin bush.

A guy walked into a travel agency and said, "I need a break from all this hustle and bustle in the city. I want to go someplace where I won't look at a human face for a week."

So the travel agent booked him into a nudist colony.

Why do men like hookers?

It's nice to have somebody working under you.

Why should you be especially nice to female executives?

You never know when they'll have an opening you could fill.

———————————

The husband and wife were arguing about their sex life when the husband offered, "When I make love, I have all the fire of a volcano."

"You're a volcano, all right," the wife retorted. "Trouble is, it's about three years between eruptions."

———————————

A guy walked into a bar and sat next to a friend. As he ordered his shot and beer, he noticed a very expensively dressed, still-beautiful woman in her forties sitting alone and weeping while she knocked back drink after drink. "Who's that?" the guy asked his pal.

"That's the madam who owns the whorehouse over on Baldelli Street," the friend replied.

"So what's her beef?" the guy asked. "That place is always mobbed."

"You might say it's a question of charity. She made a fortune selling pussy and now her daughter spends day and night giving it away."

Do women like Grand Prix racing?

No, most prefer hot rods.

Two old buddies went back to their college for alumni weekend. During the welcoming cocktail party, one began chatting with a very friendly and very well-built woman. Before the party was over, the couple had adjourned to a motel room.

The next morning, the unlucky alum was having breakfast in the cafeteria when his buddy stumbled in, grinning but exhausted. While they had coffee, the guy asked, "When did that woman you were with last night graduate?"

The second guy said, "I never asked her. But I can tell you from experience that she's the class of '69."

Why did medieval princesses hate the daytime?

They preferred a long, hard knight.

What's a legal secretary?

One that's over eighteen.

———————

A guy went to a party at a neighbor's house, met a delightful young lady, then adjourned to his apartment. The next morning, he met his neighbor while fetching the paper and said, "That friend of yours, Marla, is certainly some woman."

"She's not a friend," the neighbor replied. "She's just an acquaintance."

"Well, then," the guy said, "I'm delighted to have made your acquaintance."

———————

How can you tell if a girl is a nymphomaniac?

The writing on her T-shirt is in braille.

Chapter Nine

Simply Disgusting

A farmer was driving by the place next door when he saw the neighbor's fourteen-year-old boy standing by the wreckage of a collapsed outhouse. The farmer got out of his pickup, walked over, and heard the boy cry, "Oh, no. My pa's going to kill me."

The farmer put his arm around the lad and said, "Tell me, son. What happened?"

The boy sniffed. "I put the tractor in reverse instead of forward, and backed into the outhouse. And my pa's going to kill me."

"Son," the farmer said, "I'm sure you father's going to understand it was an accident. Now, I want you to come with me to have lunch with my missus and settle yourself down."

Reluctantly, the boy agreed. An hour later, he pushed himself away from a plate that had been heaped with roast beef, mashed potatoes, and gravy. "Ma'am," the boy said, "that sure was a wonderful dinner. But I still know my pa's going to kill me."

"For the last time," the farmer said, "you just tell your pa you backed into the outhouse by accident. How could he be mad?"

"Because he was sitting on the shitter at the time," the boy replied.

How did the Harlem Hospital cut its waste-disposal bill?

Kept a pit bull in the operating room to eat the scraps.

What is the difference between a microwave oven and anal sex?

A microwave oven won't brown your meat.

How do you know a guy is a real loser?

He calls his doctor to complain about diarrhea, and the doctor puts him on hold.

What's the most practical thing to do with the ashes after Grandma's cremated?

Put them in an Etch-A-Sketch.

What's the best way to let people know you don't like their smoking?

Carry a water pistol filled with gasoline.

Why did the eighty-year-old man molest his teen-age granddaughter?

Someone told him it isn't your age that's important, it's what age you feel.

Why is your grandma's pussy like Freddy Krueger?

One look at either one will scare the shit out of you.

Did you hear that Adolph Hitler once entered the Pillsbury Bakeoff?

His recipe began, "Set oven at 700 degrees. Add 1,000 Jews . . ."

Where do masochists meet?

At a smack bar.

How do you tell if a necrophile is gay?

He goes into the morgue and offers to lick any man in the house.

How did the necrophiliac get AIDS?

He made a grave mistake.

How does a bulemic feed her dog?

She throws up in his dish.

_____

What's love?

The myth that one cunt is different from any other cunt.

_____

Did you hear about the new sport called Mexican baseball?

You take a drink of the water, then see how fast you can make it home.

A guy forgot his briefcase one morning, so he headed back home to pick it up. To his surprise, he walked into this bedroom to see the milkman standing naked next to the bed. "What's going on here?" the guy shouted.

The milkman took one look at him, turned toward the wife lying in the bed, squatted, and said, "Listen, lady, I'll warn you again. You don't pay your bill, I'll shit on your rug."

———————

Why is it so sad being a necrophiliac?

No matter how hard you try, your love inevitably decays.

———————

What's worse than sharing a sleeping bag at summer camp?

You have to share a sleeping bag with a bed-wetter.

———————

What's worse than a kid sneezing in your face?

Having him wipe his nose on your sleeve.

What's worse than watching a kid pick his nose while you eat?

Having him flick it in your milk.

_____

How do you know they screwed up your vasectomy?

When you wake up, they've replaced your *Playboy* with *Woman's Day*.

_____

How do we know pigeons are troublemakers?

When one flies over a ballpark, the shit hits the fan.

_____

Why is it fun to drive drunk?

You run into the most interesting people.

How do you know the mosquitoes were bad at summer camp?

Your son comes home wearing a 36D bra.

Why did the wife hide ten sticks of dynamite in her birthday cake?

When she lit the candles, she and her husband finally went out together.

Why did the widower mix his wife's ashes with marijuana?

So she could make him feel good at least once in his life.

Did you hear about the sentimental necrophiliac?

He finally cremated his lover so she'd be just another piece of ash.

How do you find a girl who gives golden showers?

Follow the yellow brick road.

————————————

Why is sex with a golden-shower freak considered perverted?

Perversion begins with pee.

————————————

How do you know your kid's going to become a pervert?

He dresses up like a fire hydrant before he goes out to play with the dog.

————————————

How do you know your kid's a sadist?

He gets a girl pregnant just to kill a rabbit.

What's the new slogan of the Funeral Directors' Association?

"Our day begins when yours ends."

_____

What's ugly?

A woman who couldn't get a hickey from a leech.

_____

Did you hear that the cemetery industry is trying to upgrade its image?

Instead of peddling burial plots, they're taking advance reservations for the Home for the Permanently Still.

_____

Why is a fag like a napkin?

He's always on somebody's lap.

Did you hear about the necrophiliac with the Oedipal complex?

He'd only have sex with mummies.

Why is a kid who picks his nose like an incontinent nun?

They both have gross habits.

A very health-conscious man followed his friend through the cafeteria line and watched him load his plate with fried steak, french fried potatoes, rolls and butter, Coke, and Twinkies. When they went to the table, the man said, "Hey, you're killing yourself with all that junk. Me, I only eat natural foods."

The second guy finished a french fry, then said, "You're wrong. Natural foods have to be bad for you."

"How can you say that?"

"Because almost everybody who croaks dies of natural causes."

Did you hear about the guy who had fire insurance but no life insurance?

His wife had him cremated.

_____

Why shouldn't you douche with fluoridated water?

You'll end up without a cavity.

_____

How do you know your kid's being molested at his day-care center?

You have to play strip poker to get him in the tub.

_____

Why is chewing gum like fellatio?

It's hard to decide what to do with the wad when you're done.

BOLT IS A LOVER *AND* A FIGHTER!

BOLT
Zebra's Blockbuster Adult Western Series
by Cort Martin

WHITE SQUAW BY E. J. HUNTER

WHITE SQUAW #14   (2075, $2.50)
As Rebecca Caldwell and her trusted companion Lone
Wolf are riding back to the Dakota Territory, their train is
ambushed by angry Sioux warriors. Becky ultimately finds
out that evil Grover Ridgeway is laying claim to the land
that the Indians call their own—and decides to take Grover
in hand and pump out some information. Once she has
him firmly in line, the White Squaw blows the cover off of
his operation!

WHITE SQUAW #18   (2585, $2.95)
Hot on the heels of her long-time enemy, Roger Styles, Rebecca Caldwell is determined to whip him into shape once
and for all. Headed for San Antonio and eager for action,
Becky's more than ready to bring the lowdown thieving
Styles under thumb—especially when she discovers he's
made off with her gold. Luck seems to be on the White
Squaw's side when Styles falls into her lap—and ends up
behind bars.

WHITE SQUAW #19   (2769, $2.95)
Rebecca Caldwell was in no mood for romance after
owlhoots murdered her lover Bob Russel. But with the
rich, handsome teamster, Win Harper, standing firm and
coming on hard, Becky feels that old familiar fire rising up
once more . . . and soon the red-hot halfbreed's back in
the saddle again!

*Available wherever paperbacks are sold, or order direct from the
Publisher. Send cover price plus 50¢ per copy for mailing and
handling to Zebra Books, Dept. 3158, 475 Park Avenue South,
New York, N.Y. 10016. Residents of New York, New Jersey and
Pennsylvania must include sales tax. DO NOT SEND CASH.*